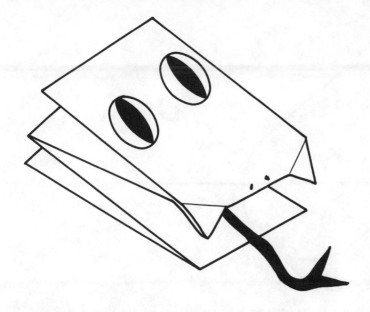

Snake

1. Make the basic folded puppet out of 9'' x 18'' (22.8 x 45.7cm) green construction paper.
2. Trace the pattern pieces on construction paper.
3. Cut out the pattern pieces.
4. Assemble as follows:

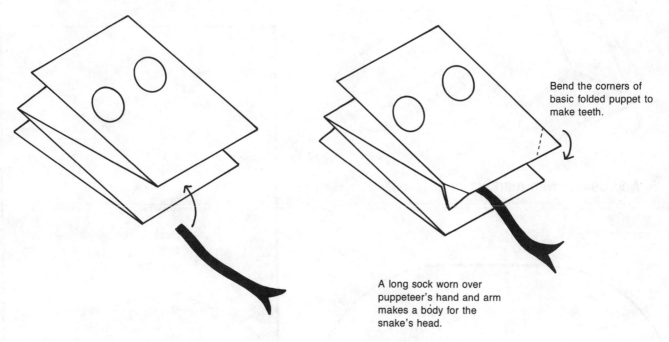

Bend the corners of basic folded puppet to make teeth.

A long sock worn over puppeteer's hand and arm makes a body for the snake's head.

5. Add details with markers or crayons.

snake eye
cut 2
yellow

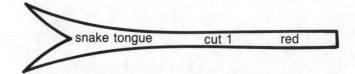

snake tongue   cut 1   red

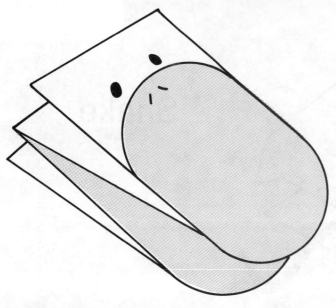

Duck

1. Make the basic folded puppet out of 9'' x 18'' (22.8 x 45.7cm) white construction paper.
2. Trace the pattern pieces on construction paper.
3. Cut out the pattern pieces.
4. Assemble as follows:

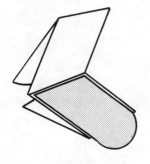 

5. Add details with markers or crayons.

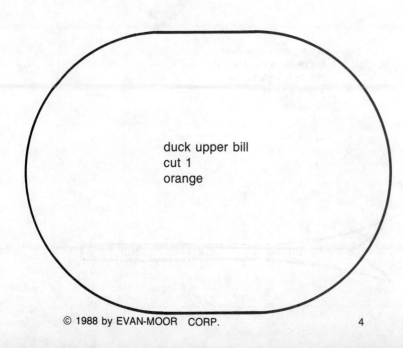

duck upper bill
cut 1
orange

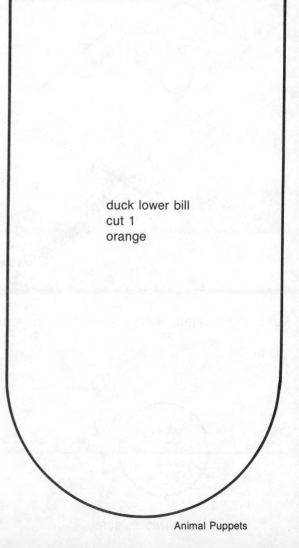

duck lower bill
cut 1
orange

4

Animal Puppets

Contents

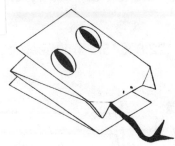

© 1988 by EVAN-MOOR CORP.

Animal Puppets

Basic Fold Directions

- Begin with a 9'' x 18'' (22.8 x 45.7cm) piece of construction paper.

- Fold in thirds lengthwise.

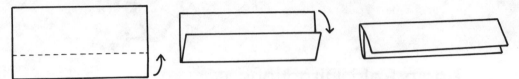

- Flip paper over.

- Fold in half.

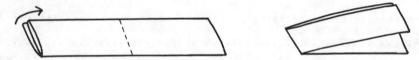

- Fold top edge back to meet fold.

- Flip over.

 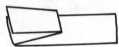

- Fold top edge back to meet fold.

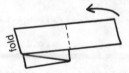

- Fingers go in open spaces.

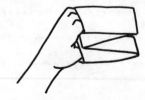

         Animal Puppets

Hippo

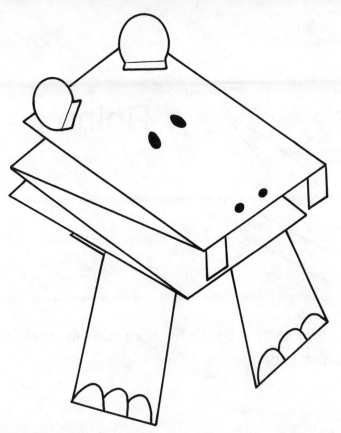

1. Make the basic folded puppet out of 9'' x 18'' (22.8 x 45.7cm) gray construction paper.
2. Trace the pattern pieces on construction paper.
3. Cut out the pattern pieces.
4. Assemble as follows:

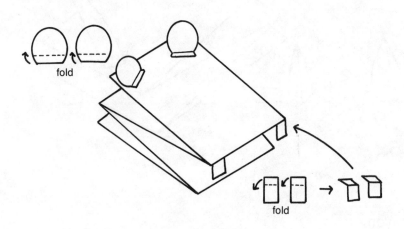

fold

fold

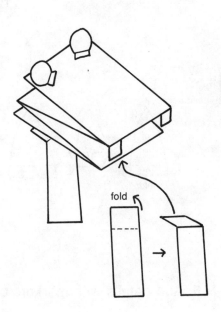

fold

5. Add details with markers or crayons.

hippo ear
cut 2
gray

hippo tooth
cut 2
white

hippo leg
cut 2
gray

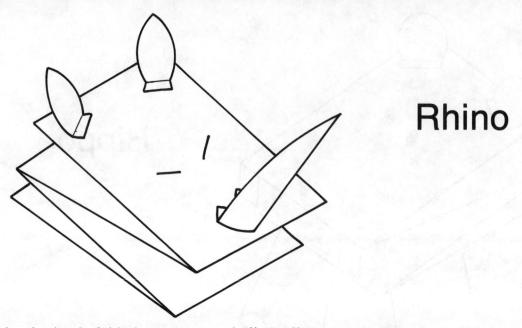

Rhino

1. Make the basic folded puppet out of 9'' x 18'' (22.8 x 45.7cm) gray construction paper.
2. Trace the pattern pieces on construction paper.
3. Cut out the pattern pieces.
4. Assemble as follows:

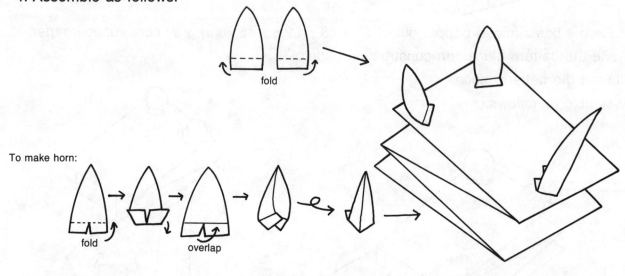

fold

To make horn:

fold   overlap

5. Add details with markers or crayons.

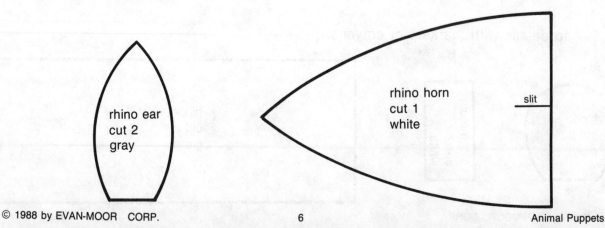

rhino ear
cut 2
gray

rhino horn
cut 1
white

slit

Animal Puppets

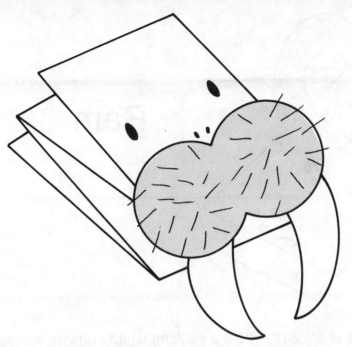

Walrus

1. Make the basic folded puppet out of 9'' x 18'' (22.8 x 45.7cm) brown construction paper.

2. Trace the pattern pieces on construction paper.

3. Cut out the pattern pieces.

4. Assemble as follows:

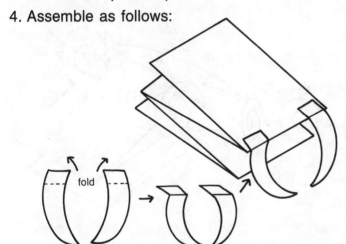

fold

5. Add details with markers or crayons.

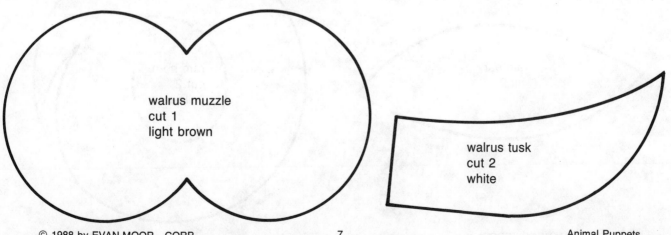

walrus muzzle
cut 1
light brown

walrus tusk
cut 2
white

Animal Puppets

Ram

1. Make the basic folded puppet out of 9'' x 18'' (22.8 x 45.7cm) white construction paper.
2. Trace the pattern pieces on construction paper.
3. Cut out the pattern pieces.
4. Assemble as follows:

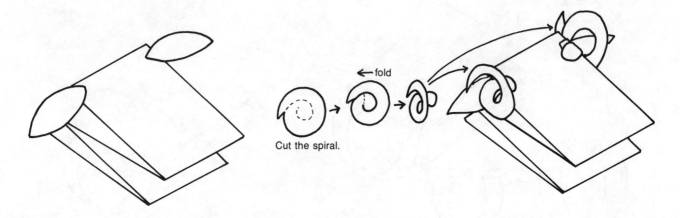

← fold

Cut the spiral.

5. Add details with markers or crayons.

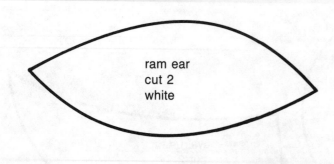

ram ear
cut 2
white

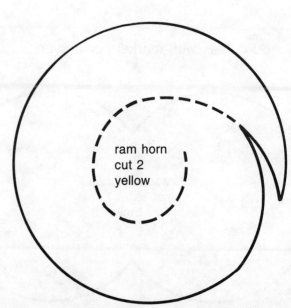

ram horn
cut 2
yellow

         Animal Puppets

Lamb

1. Make the basic folded puppet out of 9'' x 18'' (22.8 x 45.7cm) white construction paper.
2. Trace the pattern pieces on construction paper.
3. Cut out the pattern pieces.
4. Assemble as follows:

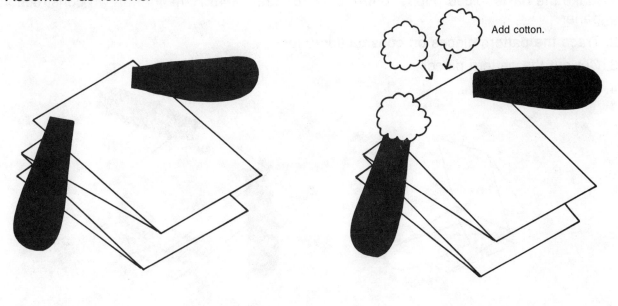

Add cotton.

5. Add details with markers or crayons.

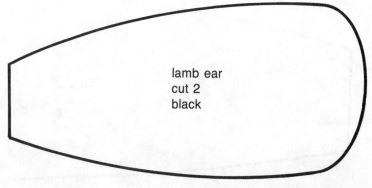

lamb ear
cut 2
black

             Animal Puppets

Dog

1. Make the basic folded puppet out of 9'' x 18'' (22.8 x 45.7cm) light brown construction paper.

2. Trace the pattern pieces on construction paper.

3. Cut out the pattern pieces.

4. Assemble as follows:

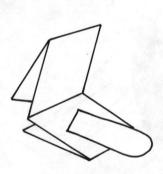 

5. Add details with markers or crayons.

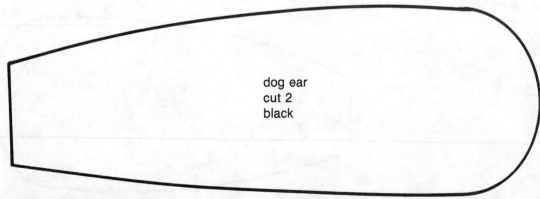

dog ear
cut 2
black

Animal Puppets

Dog Pattern

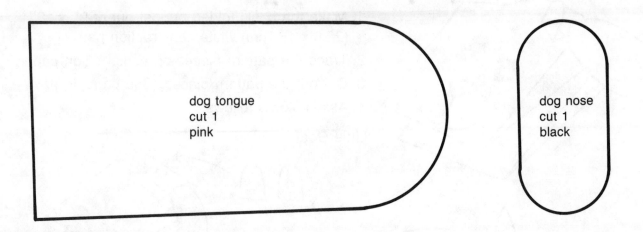

dog tongue
cut 1
pink

dog nose
cut 1
black

Goat Pattern

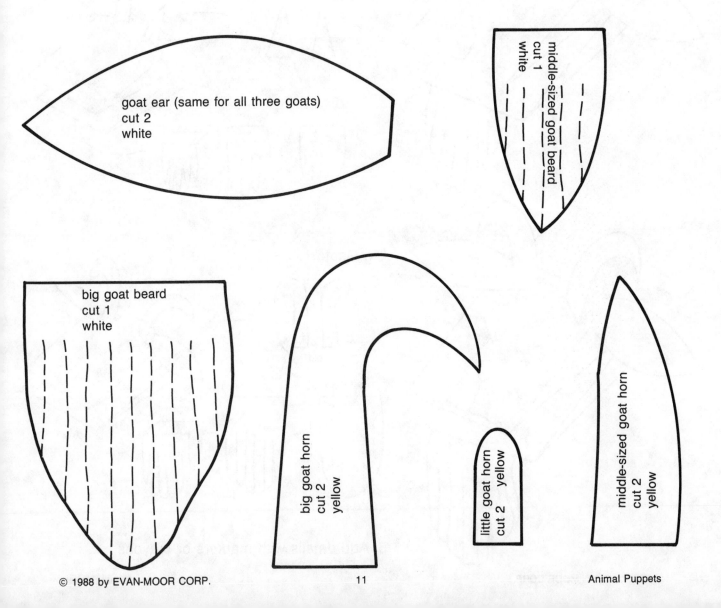

goat ear (same for all three goats)
cut 2
white

middle-sized goat beard
cut 1
white

big goat beard
cut 1
white

big goat horn
cut 2
yellow

little goat horn
cut 2   yellow

middle-sized goat horn
cut 2
yellow

Animal Puppets

Goats

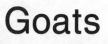

1. Make the basic folded puppet out of 9" x 18" (22.8 x 45.7cm) white construction paper.
2. Trace the pattern pieces on construction paper.
3. Cut out the pattern pieces. (See page 11.)
4. Assemble as follows:

Little Goat:

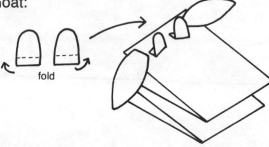

fold

Middle-Sized Goat:

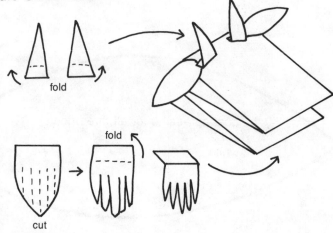

fold

fold

cut

Big Goat:

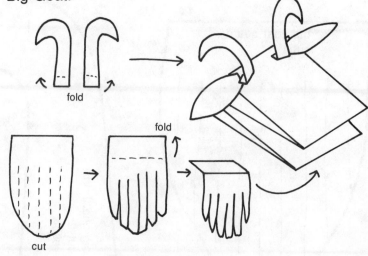

fold

fold

cut

5. Add details with markers or crayons.

Animal Puppets

Cow

1. Make the basic folded puppet out of 9'' x 18'' (22.8 x 45.7cm) brown construction paper.
2. Trace the pattern pieces on construction paper.
3. Cut out the pattern pieces.
4. Assemble as follows:

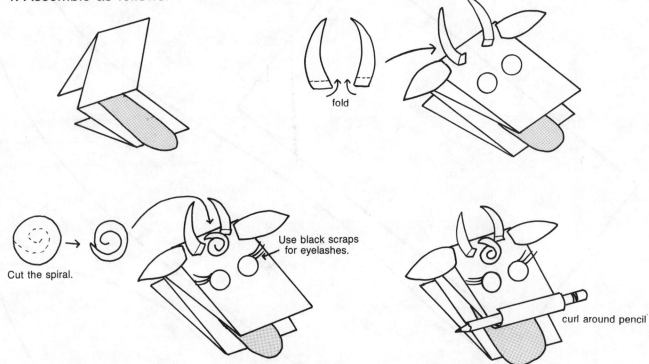

fold

Cut the spiral.

Use black scraps for eyelashes.

curl around pencil

5. Add details with markers or crayons.

         Animal Puppets

Cow Pattern

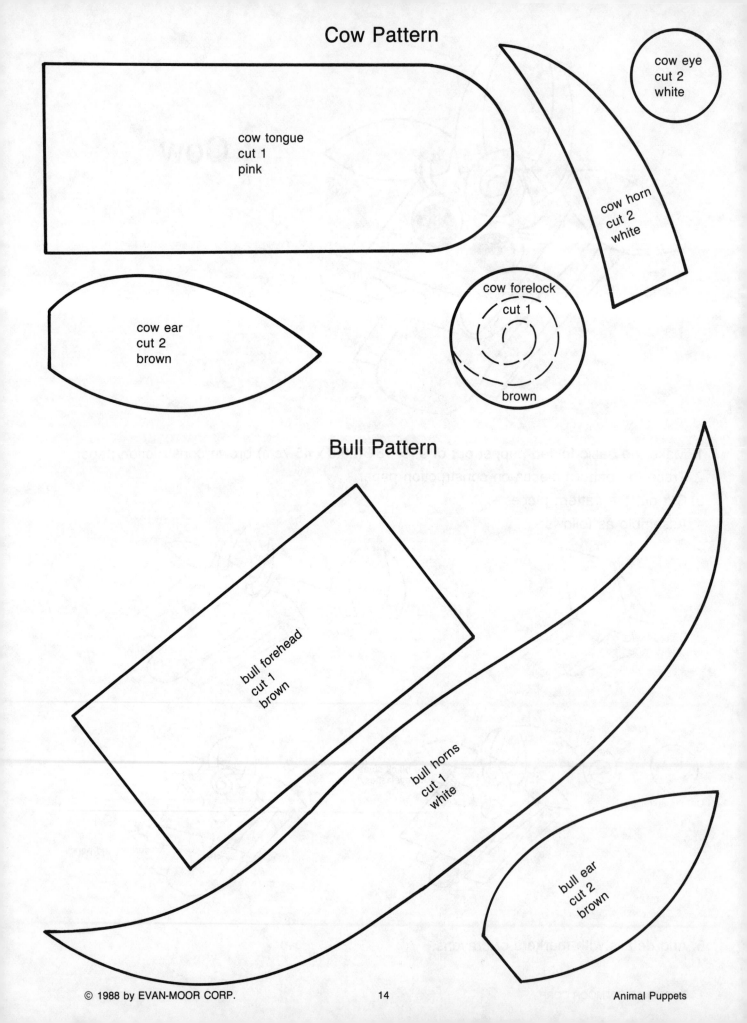

cow tongue
cut 1
pink

cow eye
cut 2
white

cow horn
cut 2
white

cow ear
cut 2
brown

cow forelock
cut 1
brown

Bull Pattern

bull forehead
cut 1
brown

bull horns
cut 1
white

bull ear
cut 2
brown

Animal Puppets

Bull

1. Make the basic folded puppet out of 9'' x 18'' (22.8 x 45.7cm) brown construction paper.
2. Trace the pattern pieces on construction paper.
3. Cut out the pattern pieces. (See page 14.)
4. Assemble as follows:

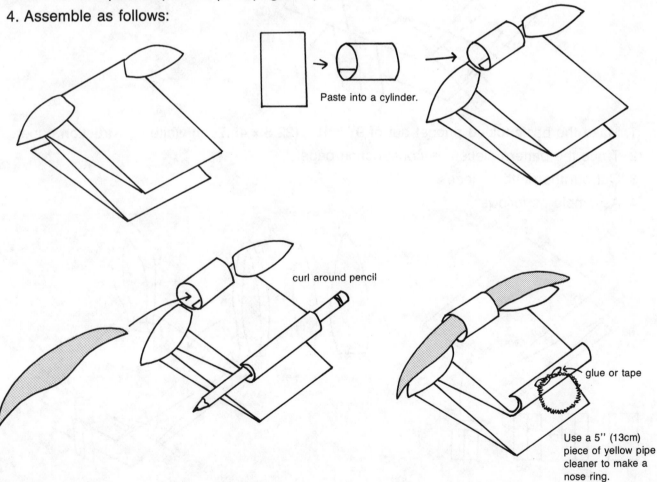

Paste into a cylinder.

curl around pencil

glue or tape

Use a 5'' (13cm) piece of yellow pipe cleaner to make a nose ring.

5. Add details with markers or crayons.

                   Animal Puppets

Rabbit

1. Make the basic folded puppet out of 9'' x 18'' (22.8 x 45.7cm) white construction paper.

2. Trace the pattern pieces on construction paper.

3. Cut out the pattern pieces.

4. Assemble as follows:

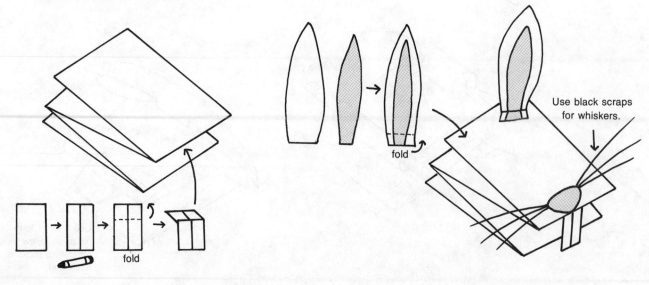

fold

Use black scraps for whiskers.

fold

5. Add details with markers or crayons.

       Animal Puppets

Rabbit Pattern

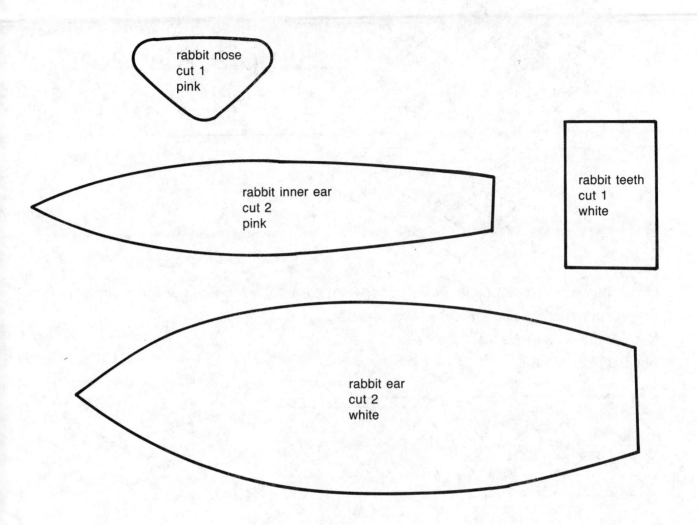

rabbit nose
cut 1
pink

rabbit inner ear
cut 2
pink

rabbit teeth
cut 1
white

rabbit ear
cut 2
white

Simple Alligator Pattern

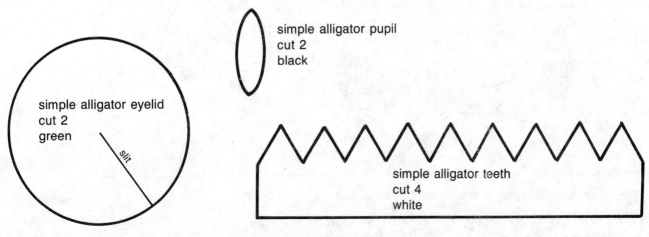

simple alligator pupil
cut 2
black

simple alligator eyelid
cut 2
green

slit

simple alligator teeth
cut 4
white

Animal Puppets

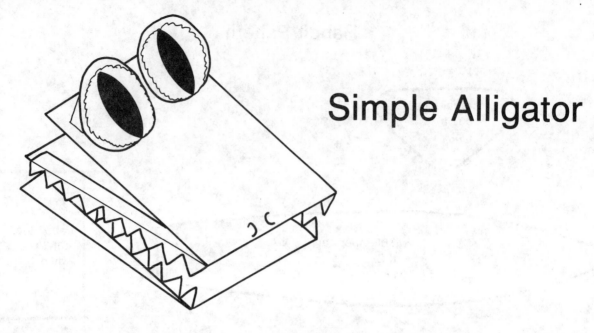

Simple Alligator

1. Make the basic folded puppet out of 9'' x 18'' (22.8 x 45.7cm) green construction paper.
2. Trace the pattern pieces on construction paper.
3. Cut out the pattern pieces. (See page 17.)
4. Assemble as follows:

fold

overlap

Use cotton balls for whites of eyes.

5. Add details with markers or crayons.

Animal Puppets

Elaborate Alligator

Special thanks to fourth grader Jeff Morgan.

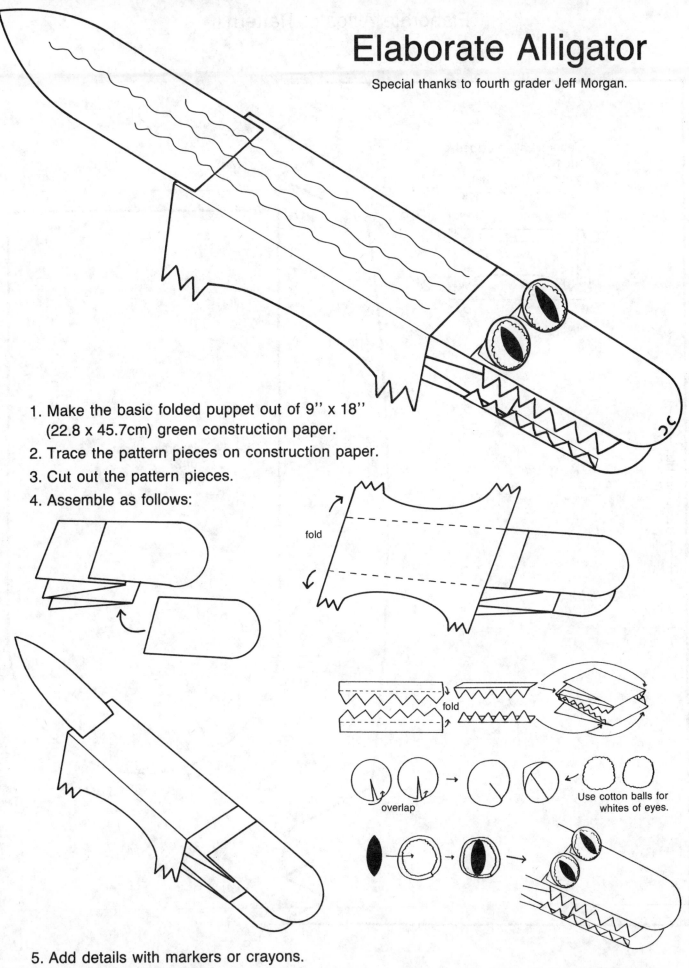

1. Make the basic folded puppet out of 9" x 18" (22.8 x 45.7cm) green construction paper.
2. Trace the pattern pieces on construction paper.
3. Cut out the pattern pieces.
4. Assemble as follows:

fold

fold

overlap

Use cotton balls for whites of eyes.

5. Add details with markers or crayons.

Animal Puppets

Elaborate Alligator Pattern

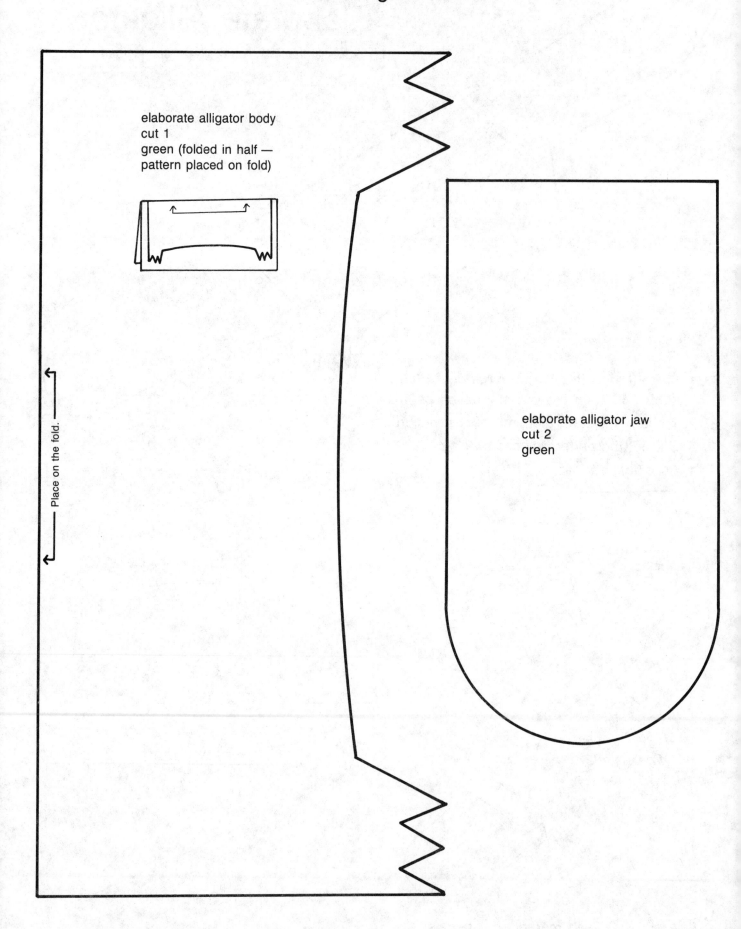

elaborate alligator body
cut 1
green (folded in half —
pattern placed on fold)

Place on the fold.

elaborate alligator jaw
cut 2
green

Animal Puppets

Elaborate Alligator Pattern

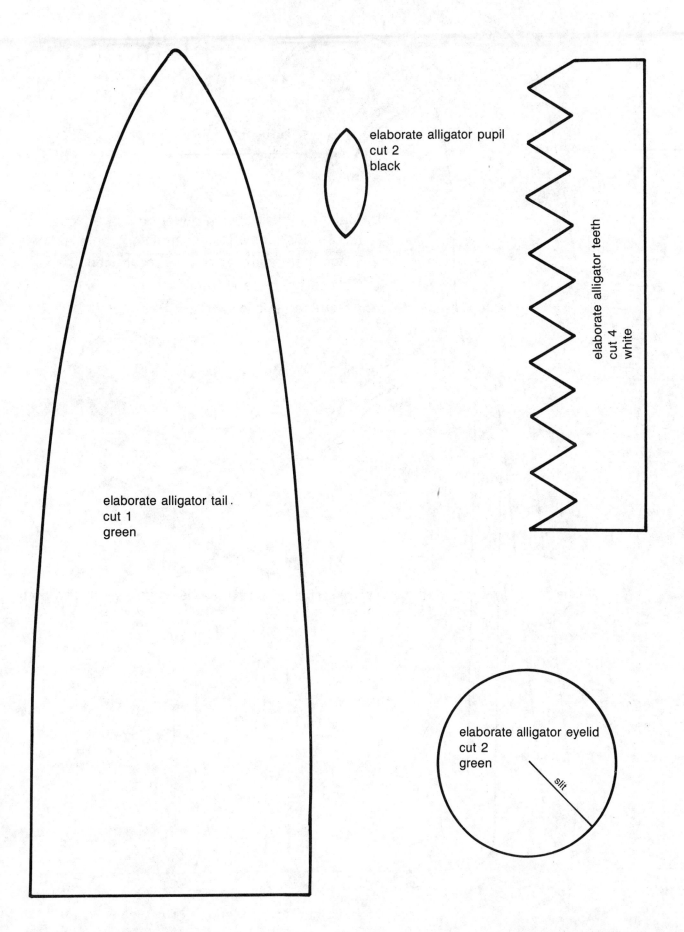

elaborate alligator pupil
cut 2
black

elaborate alligator teeth
cut 4
white

elaborate alligator tail .
cut 1
green

elaborate alligator eyelid
cut 2
green

slit

Animal Puppets

Flamingo

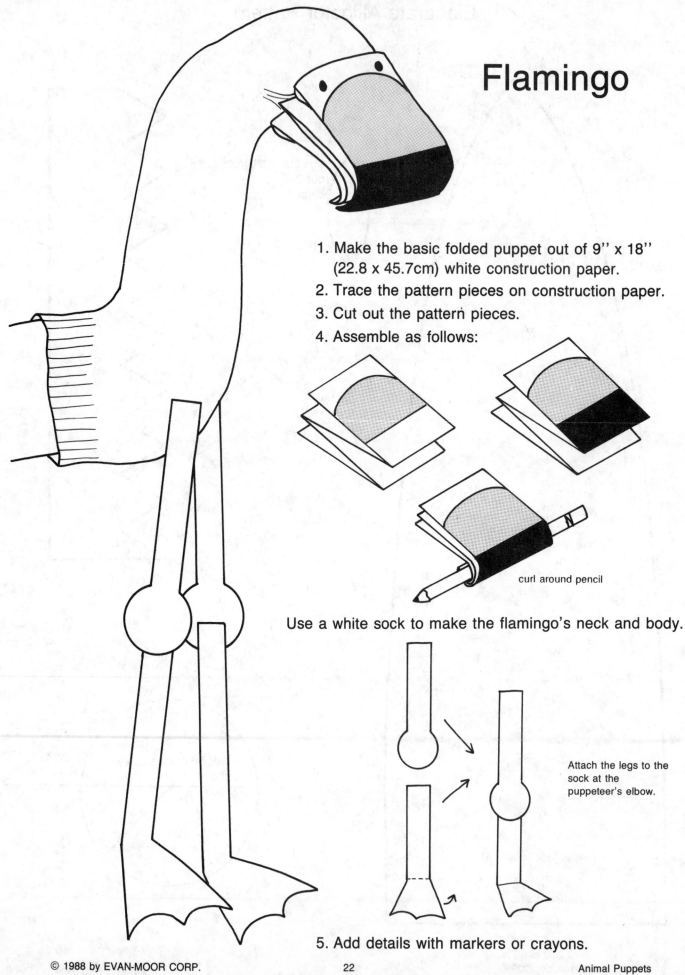

1. Make the basic folded puppet out of 9'' x 18'' (22.8 x 45.7cm) white construction paper.
2. Trace the pattern pieces on construction paper.
3. Cut out the pattern pieces.
4. Assemble as follows:

curl around pencil

Use a white sock to make the flamingo's neck and body.

Attach the legs to the sock at the puppeteer's elbow.

5. Add details with markers or crayons.

Animal Puppets

Flamingo Pattern

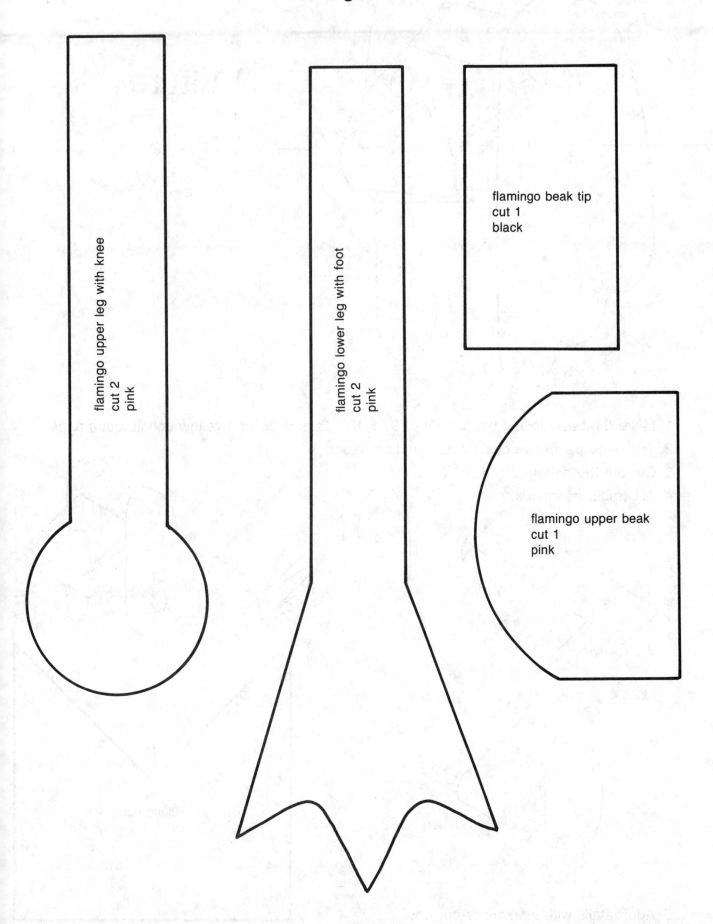

flamingo upper leg with knee
cut 2
pink

flamingo lower leg with foot
cut 2
pink

flamingo beak tip
cut 1
black

flamingo upper beak
cut 1
pink

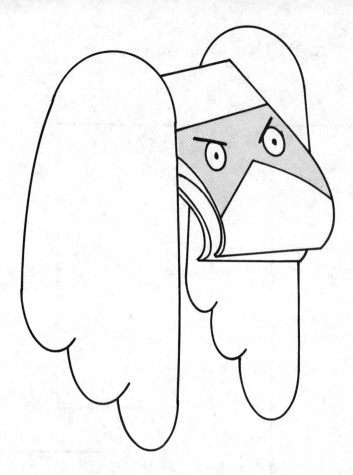

Vulture

1. Make the basic folded puppet out of 9'' x 18'' (22.8 x 45.7cm) yellow construction paper.
2. Trace the pattern pieces on construction paper.
3. Cut out the pattern pieces.
4. Assemble as follows:

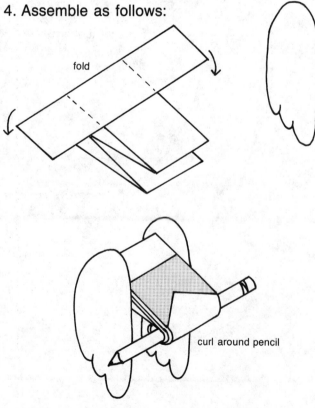

fold

curl around pencil

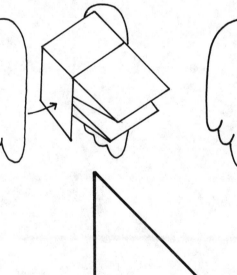

vulture head
cut 1
red

5. Add details with markers or crayons.

Vulture Pattern

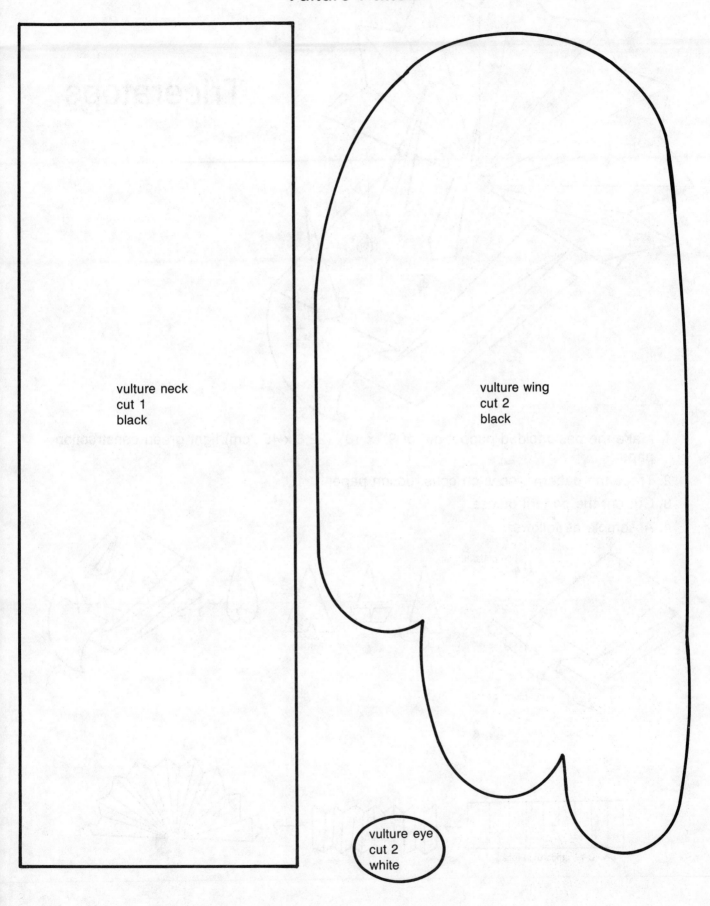

vulture neck
cut 1
black

vulture wing
cut 2
black

vulture eye
cut 2
white

Animal Puppets

Triceratops

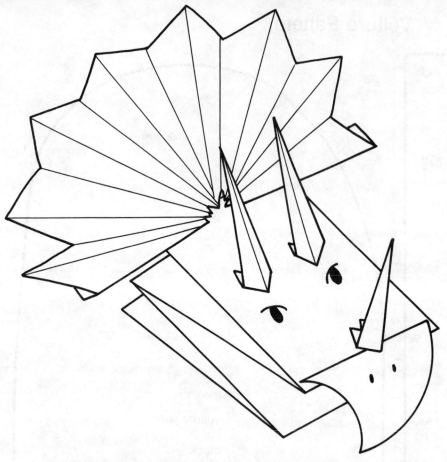

1. Make the basic folded puppet out of 9'' x 18'' (22.8 x 45.7cm) light green construction paper.

2. Trace the pattern pieces on construction paper.

3. Cut out the pattern pieces.

4. Assemble as follows:

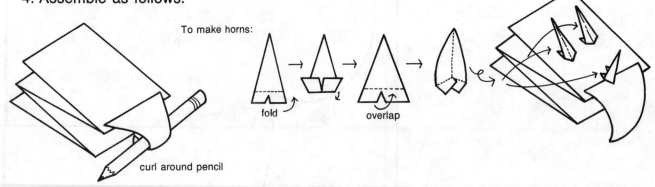

To make horns:

fold → overlap

curl around pencil

accordian fold →

5. Add details with markers or crayons.

 Animal Puppets

Triceratops Pattern

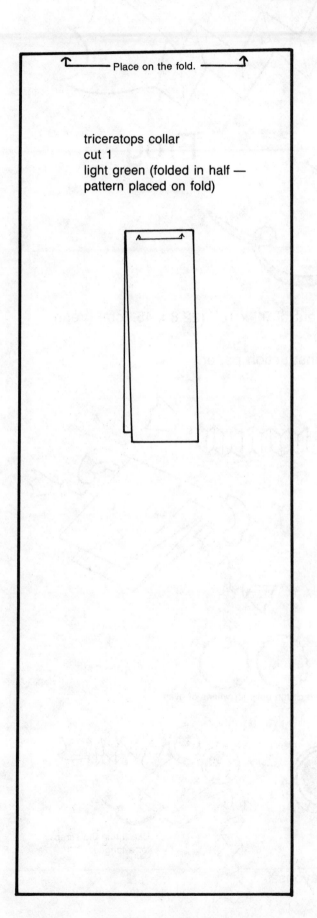

triceratops collar
cut 1
light green (folded in half —
pattern placed on fold)

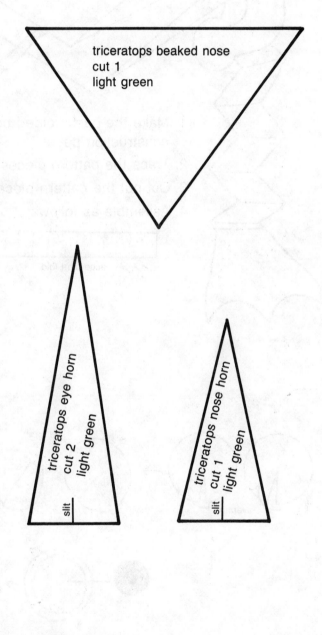

triceratops beaked nose
cut 1
light green

triceratops eye horn
cut 2
light green
slit

triceratops nose horn
cut 1
light green
slit

Animal Puppets

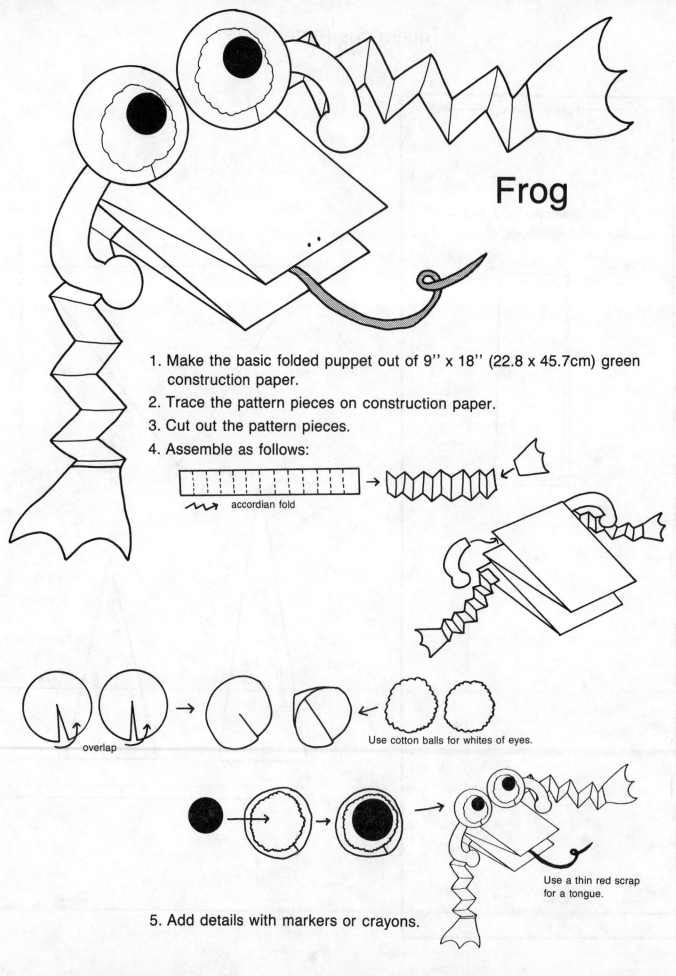

Frog

1. Make the basic folded puppet out of 9'' x 18'' (22.8 x 45.7cm) green construction paper.
2. Trace the pattern pieces on construction paper.
3. Cut out the pattern pieces.
4. Assemble as follows:

accordian fold

overlap

Use cotton balls for whites of eyes.

Use a thin red scrap for a tongue.

5. Add details with markers or crayons.

Animal Puppets

Frog Pattern

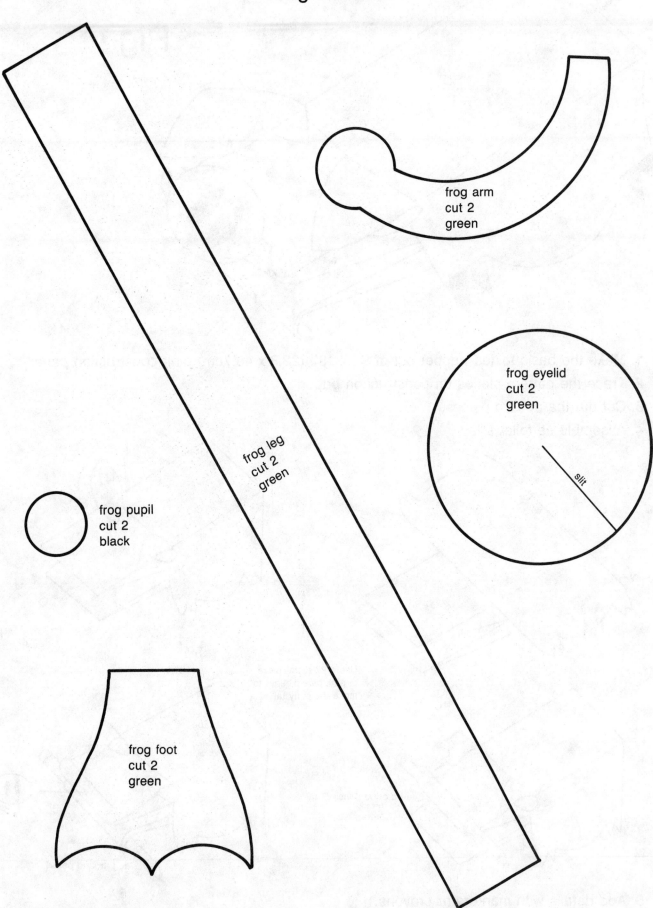

frog arm
cut 2
green

frog eyelid
cut 2
green

slit

frog leg
cut 2
green

frog pupil
cut 2
black

frog foot
cut 2
green

Animal Puppets

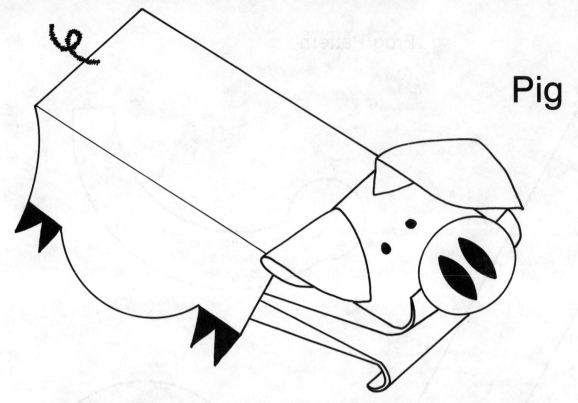

Pig

1. Make the basic folded puppet out of 9'' x 18'' (22.8 x 45.7cm) pink construction paper.
2. Trace the pattern pieces on construction paper.
3. Cut out the pattern pieces.
4. Assemble as follows:

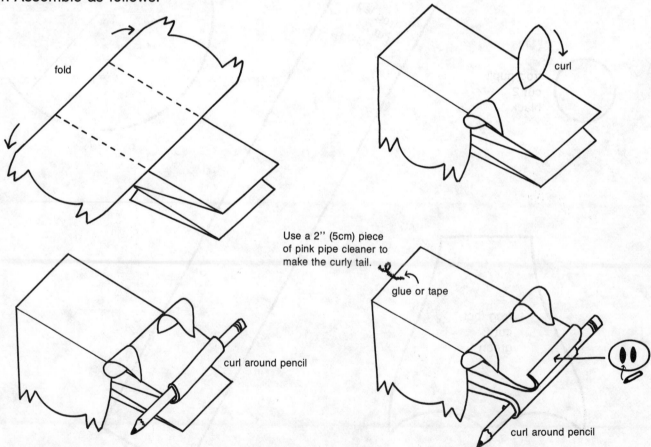

fold

curl

Use a 2'' (5cm) piece
of pink pipe cleaner to
make the curly tail.

glue or tape

curl around pencil

curl around pencil

5. Add details with markers or crayons.

Animal Puppets

Pig Pattern

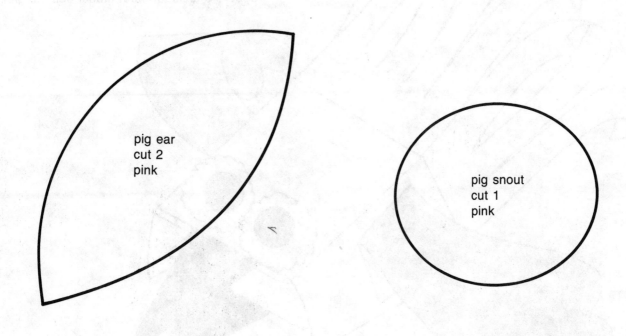

pig ear
cut 2
pink

pig snout
cut 1
pink

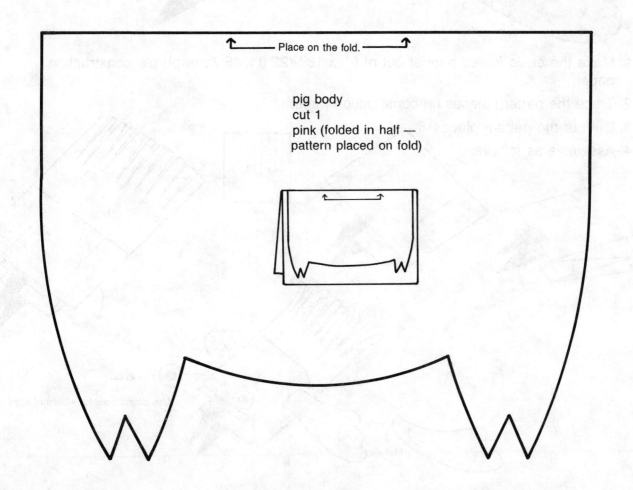

◄——— Place on the fold. ———►

pig body
cut 1
pink (folded in half —
pattern placed on fold)

Animal Puppets

Tropical Bird

Special thanks to fourth grader Jeff Morgan.

1. Make the basic folded puppet out of 9'' x 18'' (22.8 x 45.7cm) purple construction paper.
2. Trace the pattern pieces on construction paper.
3. Cut out the pattern pieces.
4. Assemble as follows:

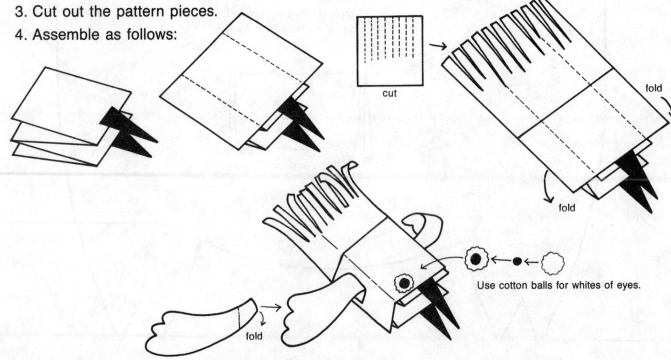

cut

fold

fold

fold

Use cotton balls for whites of eyes.

5. Add details with markers or crayons.

Animal Puppets

Tropical Bird Pattern

tropical bird body
cut 1
red

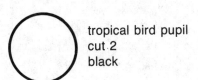

tropical bird pupil
cut 2
black

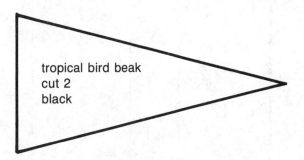

tropical bird beak
cut 2
black

 Animal Puppets

Tropical Bird Pattern

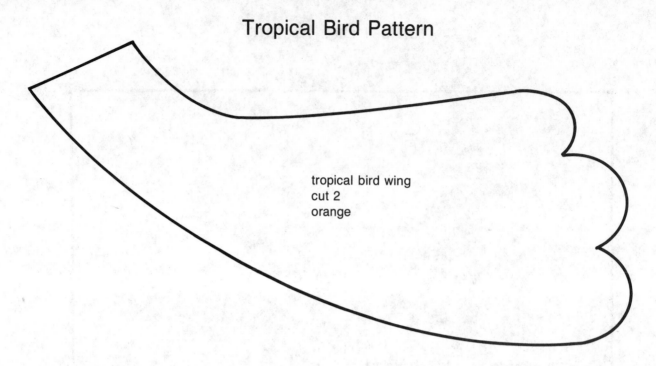

tropical bird wing
cut 2
orange

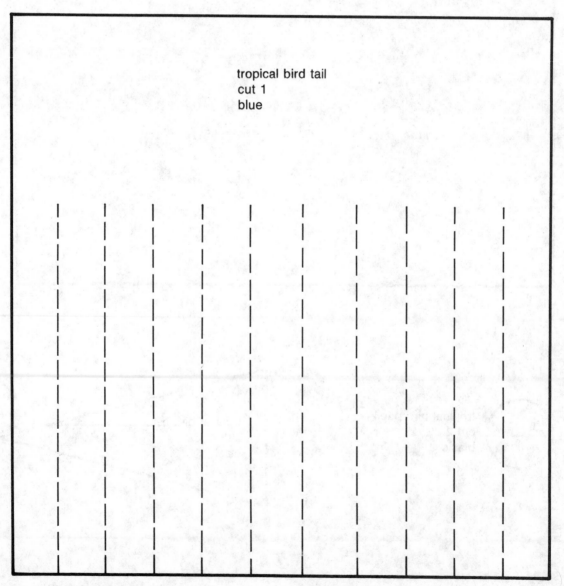

tropical bird tail
cut 1
blue

Animal Puppets

Beaver

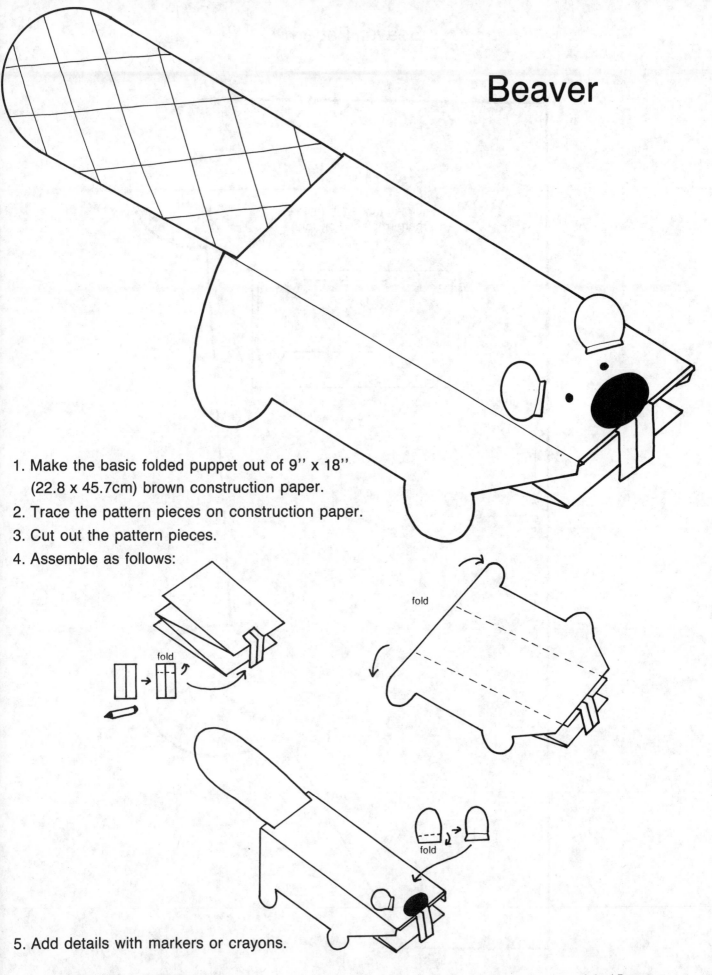

1. Make the basic folded puppet out of 9'' x 18'' (22.8 x 45.7cm) brown construction paper.

2. Trace the pattern pieces on construction paper.

3. Cut out the pattern pieces.

4. Assemble as follows:

fold

fold

fold

5. Add details with markers or crayons.

Animal Puppets

Beaver Pattern

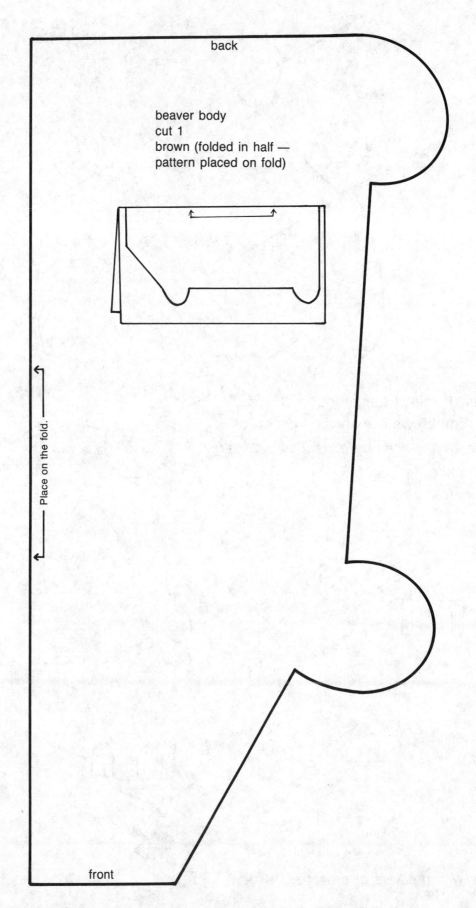

back

beaver body
cut 1
brown (folded in half —
pattern placed on fold)

Place on the fold.

front

Animal Puppets

Beaver Pattern

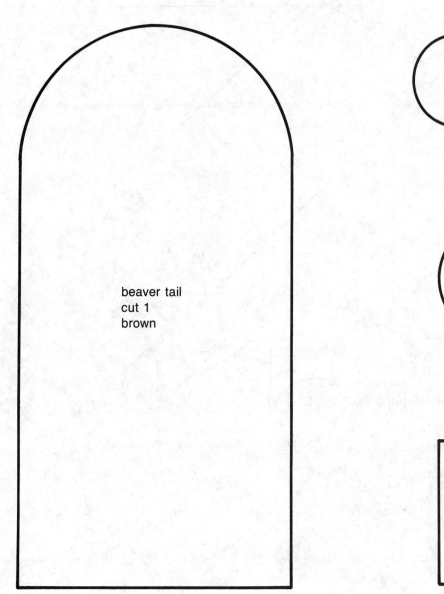

beaver nose
cut 1
black

beaver ear
cut 2
brown

beaver tail
cut 1
brown

beaver teeth
cut 1
white

Platypus

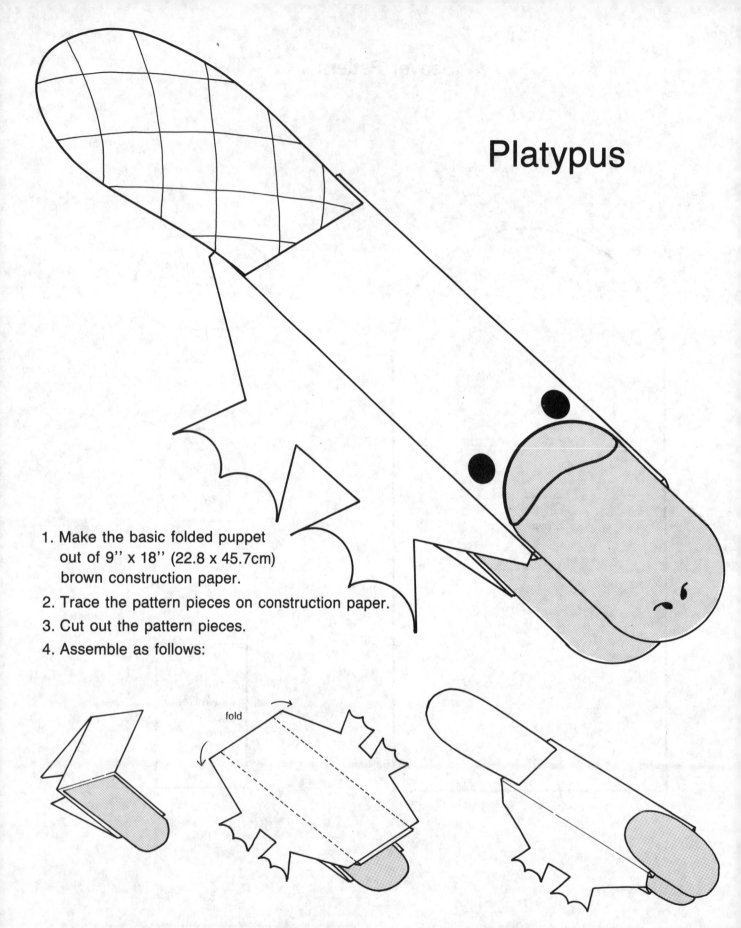

1. Make the basic folded puppet out of 9'' x 18'' (22.8 x 45.7cm) brown construction paper.

2. Trace the pattern pieces on construction paper.

3. Cut out the pattern pieces.

4. Assemble as follows:

fold

5. Add details with markers or crayons.

Animal Puppets

Platypus Pattern

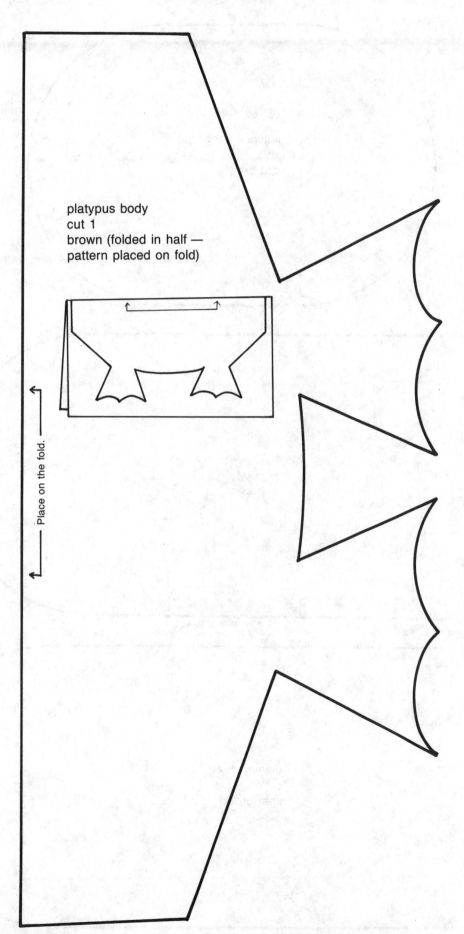

platypus body
cut 1
brown (folded in half —
pattern placed on fold)

Place on the fold.

Platypus Pattern

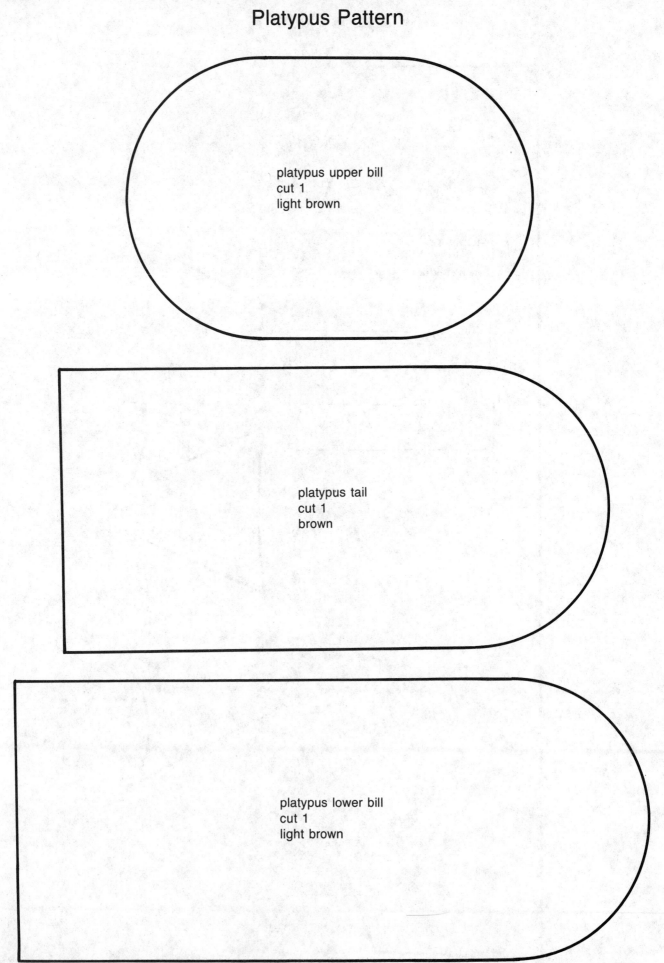

platypus upper bill
cut 1
light brown

platypus tail
cut 1
brown

platypus lower bill
cut 1
light brown

 Animal Puppets

Elephant

Special thanks to fourth grader Jeff Morgan.

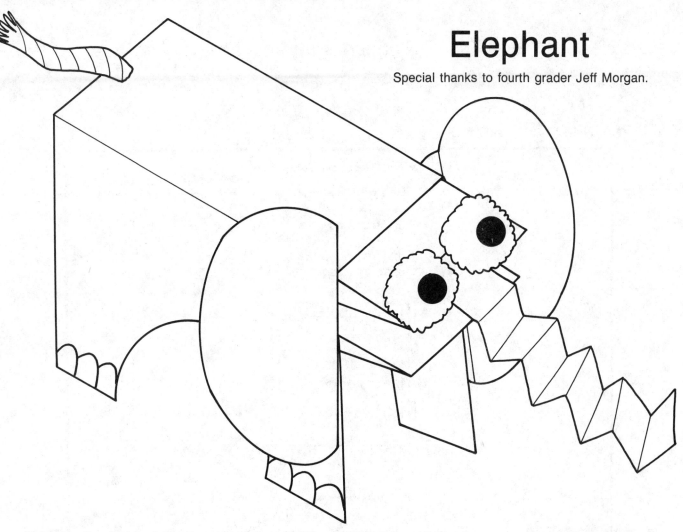

1. Make the basic folded puppet out of 9'' x 18'' (22.8 x 45.7cm) gray construction paper.
2. Trace the pattern pieces on construction paper.
3. Cut out the pattern pieces.
4. Assemble as follows:

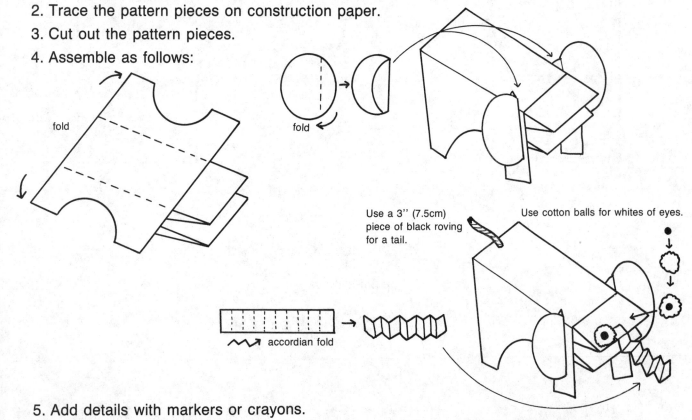

fold

fold

Use a 3'' (7.5cm) piece of black roving for a tail.

Use cotton balls for whites of eyes.

accordian fold

5. Add details with markers or crayons.

Animal Puppets

Elephant Pattern

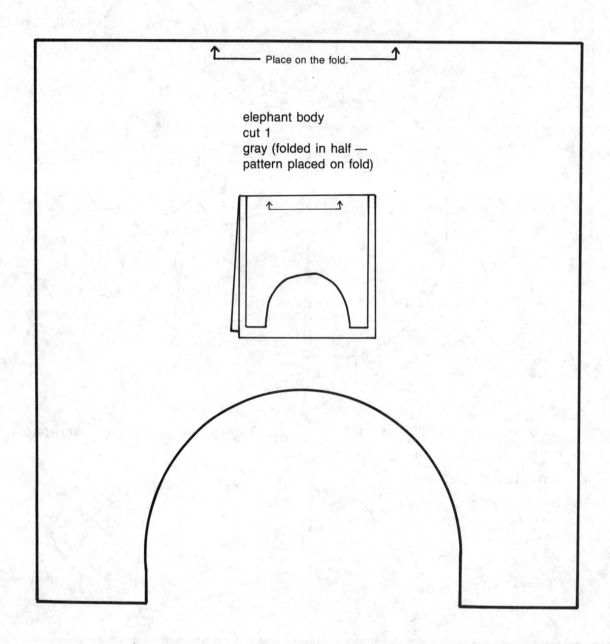

Place on the fold.

elephant body
cut 1
gray (folded in half —
pattern placed on fold)

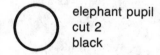

elephant pupil
cut 2
black

Animal Puppets

Elephant Pattern

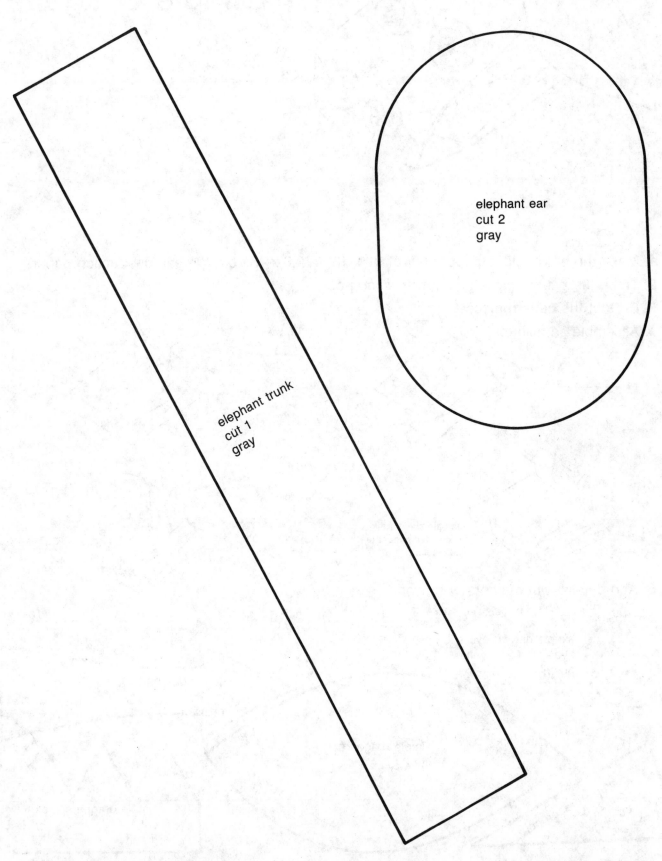

elephant ear
cut 2
gray

elephant trunk
cut 1
gray

Animal Puppets

Simple Dragon

1. Make the basic folded puppet out of 9'' x 18'' (22.8 x 45.7cm) green construction paper.
2. Trace the pattern pieces on construction paper.
3. Cut out the pattern pieces.
4. Assemble as follows:

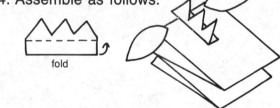

fold

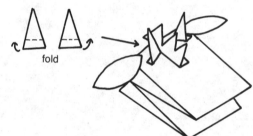

fold

Bend the corners of basic folded puppet to make teeth.

Cut the spiral.

5. Add details with markers or crayons.

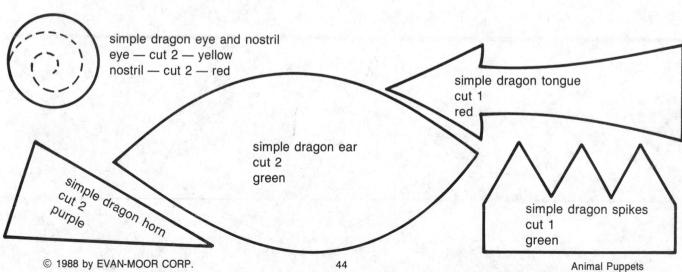

simple dragon eye and nostril
eye — cut 2 — yellow
nostril — cut 2 — red

simple dragon tongue
cut 1
red

simple dragon ear
cut 2
green

simple dragon horn
cut 2
purple

simple dragon spikes
cut 1
green

Animal Puppets

Elaborate Dragon

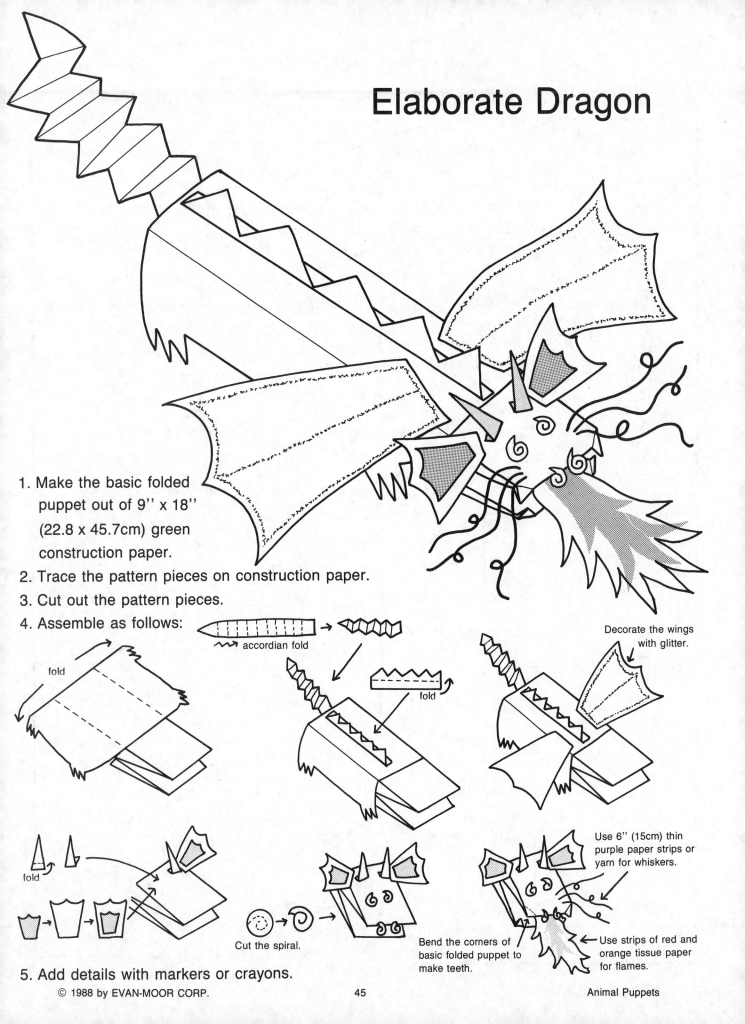

1. Make the basic folded puppet out of 9'' x 18'' (22.8 x 45.7cm) green construction paper.

2. Trace the pattern pieces on construction paper.

3. Cut out the pattern pieces.

4. Assemble as follows:

accordian fold

fold

fold

Decorate the wings with glitter.

fold

Cut the spiral.

Bend the corners of basic folded puppet to make teeth.

Use 6'' (15cm) thin purple paper strips or yarn for whiskers.

Use strips of red and orange tissue paper for flames.

5. Add details with markers or crayons.

Animal Puppets

Elaborate Dragon Pattern

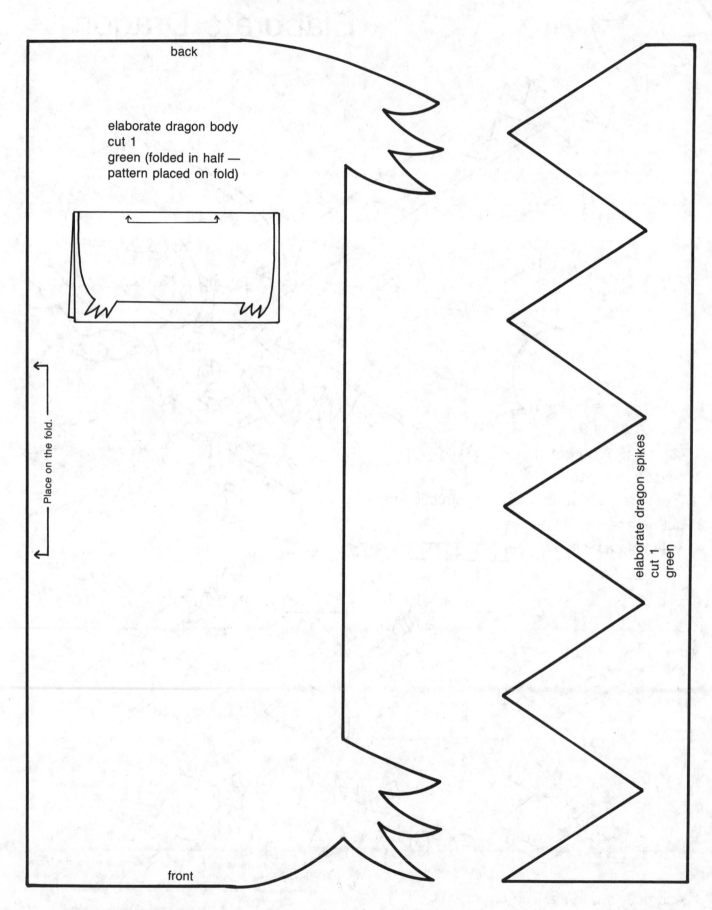

back

elaborate dragon body
cut 1
green (folded in half —
pattern placed on fold)

← Place on the fold. →

elaborate dragon spikes
cut 1
green

front

Animal Puppets

Elaborate Dragon Pattern

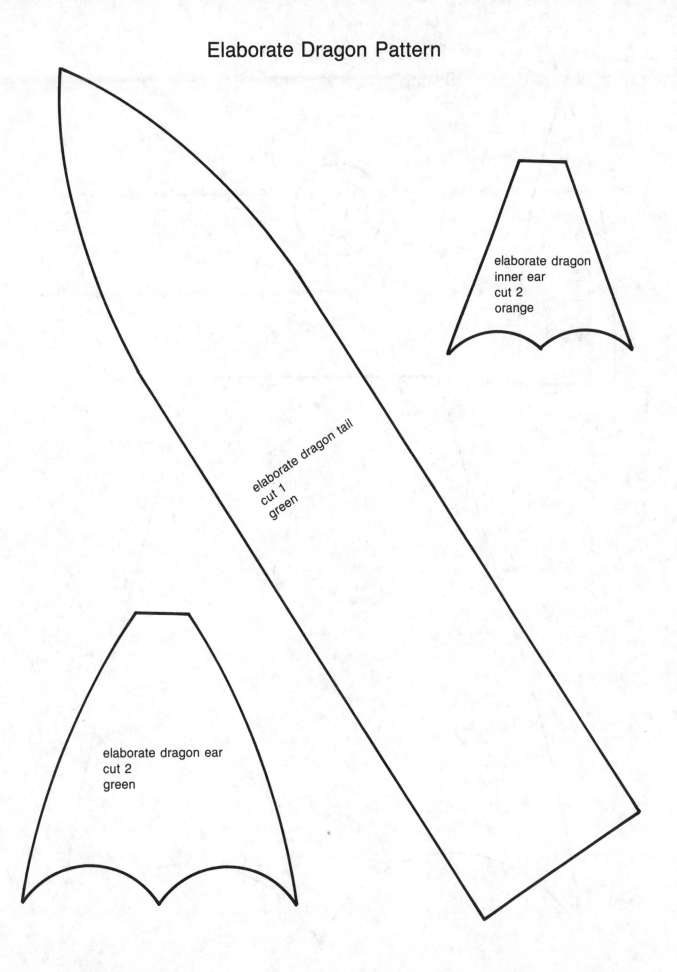

elaborate dragon
inner ear
cut 2
orange

elaborate dragon tail
cut 1
green

elaborate dragon ear
cut 2
green

47   Animal Puppets

Elaborate Dragon Pattern

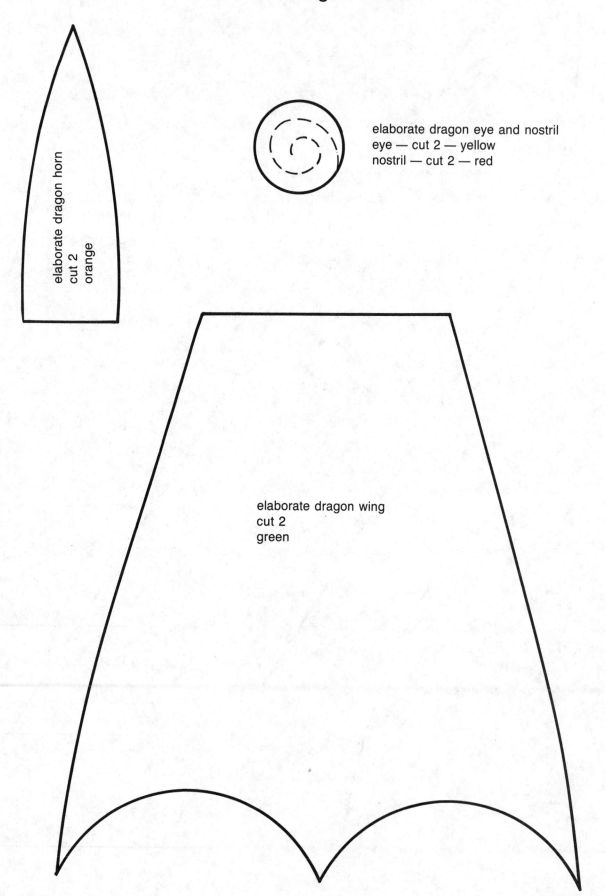

elaborate dragon horn
cut 2
orange

elaborate dragon eye and nostril
eye — cut 2 — yellow
nostril — cut 2 — red

elaborate dragon wing
cut 2
green

Animal Puppets